The A-1 Skyraider

by Steve Birdsall

ARCO PUBLISHING CO., INC.
219 PARK AVE. SOUTH, NEW YORK, N. Y. 10003

Acknowledgment

WHEN I started on this book, the A-1s were still in twelve of the fifteen Attack Carrier Air Wings. They were fighting with the Air Force and the VNAF, and were being called the most effective *COIN* aircraft we had. Then there were the MiG kills, Medal of Honor, and finally the Navy retirement.

But the Spad is not dead yet, and an obituary of BuNos and dates would be premature. If this book gives satisfaction to anyone who has been associated with the Skyraider as flyer, builder or maintainer, or, like myself, wishes he was, I will be satisfied. And, as time goes by, the book reminds one old Air Boss of the days when he used to bellow "Start the props" as well as "Start the jets," again I will be satisfied.

While concessions have been made in the area of completeness, I have tried to assure that none have been made in the area of accuracy, and I hope that the book will contribute to the eventual telling of the Skyraider's complete story. If so, it will be due to the generosity of many people. In the early stages, Crosby Maynard of Douglas and Tom Foxworth sent along enough fine material to lay the foundations. In South Vietnam and on Yankee Station, Rear Admiral Thomas J. Walker, Colonel Frank Doyal, Colonel Orley B. Caudill, Captain Jay Kane, Colonel Al Lynn, Commander Don Stone, Commander Robert R. Worchesek, Lieutenant John Lee, and many others paved the way for me and made my job easy. Tom Hansen and Lieutenant Colonel Robert A. Webb and his gracious staff supplied some superb A-1 photographs, Bob Webb as usual responded to every improbable request. The pilots — Bernie Fisher, John Shone, Les Hewitt, Glenn Givens, and the men of VA-52 — deserve and have my thanks, as do Maurice Salbert, M. R. Fowler, Captain J. H. McCurtain, Lieutenant Colonel William A. Day, Lieutenant Colonel Gerald Holland, and all those who have sent along photographs, not least Bettie Sprigg and Mrs. Virginia Fincik of ACIC. And Major Charles E. Rogers and the rest of "C" Flight, 1st Air Commandos, with whom I spent some enjoyable evenings entertained by a lot of anecdotes, some regrettably unsuitable for publication, along with a lot of details about flying the Skyraider. I thank them all and hope they enjoy this book.

Also I would like to acknowledge my wife Sandra, and my mother, Marjorie Birdsall, who typed the final manuscript after it was edited, my mentor Mrs. Phyllis Wilkie, and my brother Graham, who came up with some very necessary last minute pictures in a rather unusual way.

Steve Birdsall
Sydney, Australia

Published by ARCO PUBLISHING COMPANY, INC.
219 Park Avenue South, New York, N.Y. 10003

Library of Congress Catalog Number 70-103079
Printed in the United States of America

ISBN 0-668-02188-8

CONTENTS

About the Author...

Steve Birdsall was captivated by the A-1's business-like looks on board the U.S.S. *Coral Sea* in May 1963. Since then he has gathered material, as it came, with the intention of someday writing a Skyraider book, although he is more at home working on books like *The B-17 Flying Fortress* and *The B-24 Liberator*. In 1967 he went to Vietnam as a war correspondent for an Australian magazine and flew with the 1st Air Commandos at Pleiku and talked with Navy and VNAF pilots. That trip is what provided the basis for this book.

Foreword

IT was a hot, humid day in 1965 when I drove into Hurlburt Field, Florida for my initial introduction to the A-1 Skyraider. Past the snappy Air Force Guard—past the chapel where we would reverently bow our heads in sorrow for friends who lost their lives in training—and on to Fighter Operations where for the next two months our group would be cast together as a pilot/aircraft team. During that time, we sort of adopted a motto which has remained with me through the years—an acrostic which epitomizes my feelings for the A-1 -TISH—TOGETHER IN SERVICE AND HONOR.

I vividly recall the startling contrast between the slender, graceful F-104 Starfighter jet I had just left, a sleek and impressive queen of the air—and the oil-smudged, sturdy prop-driven Skyraider. On my very first flight in the A-1, I was impressed with her performance and felt she was unsurpassed in accuracy and reliability. Little did I dream at that time that her unique versatility and strength would make its mark in history! Although our training at Hurlburt was brief, all the pilots seemed to share my love and respect for this craft. We felt that few aircraft could compete with her for dependability, and we flew her with pride.

The admiration from the ground troops for this airplane has probably never been equaled. Her sturdy Navy landing gear amazed many of us for its ability to remain intact during the most punishing landings. The versatile and varying selections of weapons deployment were highly revered by the air crews. The outstanding endurance during close air support, the tough resistance during ground fire, her ability to carry and accurately deliver ordnance—all these qualities proved to be great assets in a jungle conflict.

In combat, the Skyraider seemed to be almost a living thing. She would quiver and groan in times of stress; she would sigh when the tension eased. When it seemed that both pilot and plane were completely exhausted, she would somehow summon up a little extra strength and transmit this confidence to the man. "We can do it—together," she would seem to say. Numerous occasions arose in the Vietnam struggle for the Skyraider to "show her stuff"—and you know, an odd thing happened. To the First Air Commandos in Vietnam, she came to look even beautiful. There was a sort of magic about her—an aura of success. We would bring her back from a combat mission ready to slide into home plate—and find ourselves hopping like a grasshopper on that unbelievably staunch gear. She was exuberant, she was irrepressible, she was inspiring.

Following a combat mission near Qui-Nhon, South Vietnam, we pilots gathered in the briefing room to discuss the results achieved, and to relax. The fighting had been hot and heavy in that area. Much to our surprise, we noted an Army Major sitting quietly in a corner. He was obviously laboring under some severe emotional stress, as his eyes seemed to be tear-filled. Suddenly he broke the silence. "I wanted to come and thank you pilots personally for all your help. Our unit was hopelessly pinned down by the enemy, and had it not been for your Skyraiders, possibly none of us would have survived." His voice broke, and now the tears flowed freely. The Major did not apologize for his emotions. "I can't help thinking of all my buddies who didn't make it." Not a word was spoken after the Major left the room. We all just looked at each other, with that warm, close camaraderie which has bound us together. Somehow I knew that each one of us was resolving to try just a little harder next time. That was the spirit of the A-1 Skyraider and of the men who flew her.

I know that my fellow pilots of the First Air Commandos would gladly join me in a salute—To the Old Faithful of the Skies—the A-1 Skyraider. Long may she reign!

BERNARD F. FISHER, Lieutenant Colonel, USAF

1. To War in a Relic

Captain Glenn G. Givens, 1st Air Commandos.

"PASSENGERS manifested on Flight 651 to Pleiku, Da Nang, Hue, and Cam Ranh Bay form a single line at the terminal exit for immediate departure. You are reminded that there is no smoking between the terminal and the aircraft, and no picture taking on the flight line. All weapons must be cleared and no flammables, grenades or explosives are permitted on the aircraft."

After having made this announcement in English, the big, broad-chested U. S. airman attempted the same in sing-song Vietnamese.

Tan Son Nhut, the world's busiest airport, was a memorable experience in itself. Check-in time for Mission 651, the second of four daily flights to points north of Saigon, was 5:45.

As we formed a single file with boarding passes in our hands, we shuffled past an unused counter, unchanged since this terminal became the 8th Aerial Port, the military terminal at Tan Son Nhut. On the wall was a curling Air Vietnam poster printed in English, that pointed out the beauties of lovely Da Nang, and tranquil, picturesque Hue, the old provincial capital.

Again the C-130's engines lulled me to sleep. Then the tires of the Hercules bit, the four engines reversed, the huge loading ramp opened, blurred by my lazy eyelids. I still felt drowsy. Some people found it impossible to sleep on the lumbering, camouflaged transports; others, like myself, were lulled to sleep by the hypnotic drone of the engines.

Join the Air Force and fly a 1945 Navy plane . . . A-1E 52-132444 at Sheppard AFB in July 1966.
(Merle Olmsted)

A sign read "Welcome to Pleiku." In the Central Highlands of South Vietnam, Pleiku is the home of the 1st Air Commando Squadron, an outfit originally formed in Burma during World War II to support Wingate's forces. Until a few days before my arrival, the commander had been Colonel Eugene Deatrick. A veteran of some 349 A-1E missions, he was the man who found *Ranger* A-1 pilot Dieter Dengler following his harrowing double escape after a crash-landing in Laos on February 1; 1966.

In the 1st Air Commando revetment area there were Skyraiders hung with every imaginable kind of ordnance—rockets, bombs, napalm, CBUs, and then-classified aerial mines which Lieutenant Jim Thyng assured me were just bubble gum dispensers. All but a couple carried the almost RAF-style camouflage the Air Force has adopted in Vietnam. Several were painted with little black heart symbols—"Purple Hearts"—one for each mission when the aircraft had come back damaged. One plane had fifteen.

Of all the aircraft in South Vietnam, I wanted most to fly in the Skyraider, and Pleiku was the place to do it.

My pilot would be Captain Glenn G. Givens of Akron, Ohio, a twenty-nine year-old veteran of 300 Vietnam missions—eighty in the Skyraider, the rest as a Forward Air Controller in the Cessna O-1E.

Over a couple of cans of beer I talked to Givens about general things. How did he rate the VNAF A-1 pilots at Pleiku—he didn't feel qualified to say. They carried lighter loads, but maybe they didn't have as much ordnance at their disposal—they showed no reluctance to deliver what they had. Givens was usually shot at a couple of times a week, mostly small arms stuff, and he had only taken hits once. His most memorable mission was when they carried two six-barreled 7.62 mm. gun pods, each with 1,500 rounds, under the wings. "Fifteen seconds of red hail," was how he described it. On that day a small Special Forces patrol had been ambushed by two to three hundred VC, who had a machine gun set up about thirty feet away. The gun pods were expended and the A-1Es were strafing so close that tree limbs fell on the Special Forces troops. A FAC had located VC moving through the jungle and Givens and his wing man, all their ammunition gone, made dry passes over their heads to keep them down. Suddenly Givens looked embarrassed, and stopped, "It was just another mission really."

The mission I was to fly was scheduled for 1530, with briefing an hour before. So, as the hot afternoon settled in, I hitched a ride from the MACV Compound down the mile or more of red dirt-edged road to the Commandos' revetment area.

The first step was to organize my equipment. Survival vest, with emergency radios, strobe light, pencil flare—everything, including snake bite treatment—a parachute, and a helmet.

In the briefing room Givens introduced me to his wingman on the mission, Major Lou Weiger. On the wall of the sparse room was a pitted Chicom AK-47 automatic rifle, mounted on a board with a metal plaque: "In appreciation for outstanding air support to the 1st Battalion, 12th Infantry, 'Red Warriors'." The gun was found with several dead VC in a position that had been hit by the A-1Es during a fierce battle in November 1966.

The briefing was divided into two sections and handled by two men. First there was a briefing on our target, a suspected VC stronghold in the area where Operation Thayer II was in progress. We were told where the U. S. troops were, where to head for in the event of trouble. The target was only about sixty miles from Pleiku, so it was a short mission. Each plane was to carry six 250-pound bombs, to be dropped individually—a light load for the A-1E. Our call signs were Hobo 27 and Hobo 28. The

Skyraider 132582, still going strong nearly a year after the mission I flew with Glenn Givens. The large tail letters and buzz numbers are the only changes. *(USAF)*

9

A-1E with frag clusters and mini-guns...a devastating anti-personnel lineup. Although rows of A-1s once languished at Litchfield Park boneyard there is no surfeit of Spads. 633rd Consolidated Aircraft Maintenance, at Pleiku, takes good care of its precious planes. Once they married the front of a mortared A-1E to the aft fuselage of a wrecked VNAF A-1G. For some reason it flys faster than their other Skyraiders. *(USAF)*

Forward Air Controller would meet us there. Then came a weather briefing. All along Givens and Weiger had been taking notes.

Takeoff time approached, and we carried our gear out to the soot-stained A-1E. The seats were side by side, in front of the unused "Blue Room," a cargo passenger area immediately behind the cockpit covered by blue-tinted glass. The wing walk was slippery. The first thing was to buckle on the parachute harness, then the seat shoulder straps. Givens briefed me on how to release them, told me how to stand up in the cabin when the canopy is jettisoned and rolled out over the wing—if we got shot down. I put on my helmet, plugged the jack into my radio lead, and tested the transmit buttons and the lip mike.

The A-1E threw out a lot of smoke when the 2400-horsepower Wright R-3350 engine started up. The blades spun slowly a few times, then faster, dissolved into a blur, then became invisible. Givens warned me to duck my head when I closed my side of the canopy and we moved slowly out of the rectangular metal revetment, and swung onto the taxiway that ran parallel to the runway. Halfway along the taxiway one of a group of ground crewmen gave us a thumbs up "good hunting" sign and we returned it. To our right Pleiku's other aircraft were parked over a large area—Hercules and C-123 transports, a couple of Army Caribous, Cessnas, the 4th Air Comandos' AC-47 Spooky gun ships. At the end of the taxiway we turned onto the strip, with Weiger to our left and behind. Givens' canopy slid closed, so I ducked my head and pushed the yellow lever at my side forward. The hydraulically operated plexiglass hood moved forward and locked. Givens ran up the engine, saw me leaning back to watch Weiger's stained old aircraft, and commented over the intercom that the Skyraider "isn't very glamorous." I reply that it all depended on how you looked at it.

Gathering speed we moved down the runway, the thousand-foot markers zipping past. Then the black, tire-streaked strip fell further below us and was replaced by green, monotonous Vietnamese countryside. The A-1E seemed to climb slowly. The day was clear, hot and sunny, but there were banks of cloud around us. Weiger caught up, slipped across to our right side for some picture taking, slid his left wing right under Givens' right wing, extended the big ventral dive brake, then side-slipped out to the right and held a position above and slightly behind us.

Close to the target Givens made contact with our FAC. We watched the silvery Cessna circle lazily over the dark patch of trees, then suddenly it flipped over and down. His smoke rockets streaked into the area we were after. Givens, as leader, went in first, and I knew my moment of truth was about to come. I'd been warned that people who had never been air-sick before had been surprised by the A-1. I knew what to expect in the pullout, and got ready. The earth and sky rolled past my eyes as Givens winged over and threw the plane into a dive. The airspeed climbed and the yellow needle hit 270 as we went deeper into the twenty degree dive. One of the yellow-nosed bombs fell from under the wings, then at about 1,000 feet Givens pulled the ship out. My whole body sagged and sweat rolled down over my face from under my helmet. The effect wore off quickly, and I looked back to the cloud of thick black smoke swirling on the ground. The FAC called Weiger, and gave directions in relation to his own smoke and our accurate bomb. The other Skyraider dived down and right then I realized why, after twenty years, the USAF has resumed camouflaging their aircraft. A bomb slipped from under the wing, Weiger's aircraft zoomed up, and there was a brief flash of orange smothered quickly by gray-black smoke.

VA-65 from *Intrepid* in August 1961. Fancy-finned 400 is CAG's aircraft. This squadron and these aircraft later cruised on the nuclear-powered *Enterprise*.

Center

The water looks cold...and close, as a Marine Corps AD-4 from VMA-211 goes off the deep end. *USS Wright,* June 1954.

Bottom

When the Skyraider showed in Vietnam, what it could still do, some thought was given to re-opening the production line, but cost would have tripled.

The FAC hovered close to a hillside, told Givens: "Put the next one about between the last two bursts." He went in again, this time dropping a bomb from the left wing. Again the pressure squashed me into the seat. Weiger went in again. I felt relieved because I hadn't been affected by the maneuvers. Again Givens dived and pulled out. Then I realized I was being affected, slowly but very surely. I didn't look forward to the next three dives, but I know they were coming. The third bomb fell from the right wing, that was number five. One more. The FAC was satisfied after the final bomb—ordnance 100 per cent on target, no ground fire, some severely mauled VC trees at the very least.

So we headed back. On the way we make contact with another FAC. Givens told him he had a full load of twenty mike-mike, could he use us? "I sure can," the voice crackled through the earphones. The FAC has six VC "hootches"—grass shacks—cornered and wanted them strafed. As we went in on the first sweeping pass the plane shuddered. An orange ball, a ricochet, arched lazily in front of us, and white smoke streamed back across the wings from the cannon barrels. Givens passed over the target at fifty feet, pulled up and went around. Weiger in Hobo 28 made his first pass. Then Givens took us in again, and about 150 rounds chopped into the target area, shearing the foliage and the flimsy target. And again. There was no groundfire, no sign of enemy activity. The FAC called us off and sent us home.

We were not far from Pleiku, and the easy flying made me feel more comfortable. We orbited the field a couple of times, our landing gear down, then we were on final approach. The tires chirped and we were down and rolling smoothly. At the end of the runway ground, crewmen jumped onto the wings and removed the rounds from the breaches of the four wing cannon. Givens folded the wings up before taxiing down to the revetment area. He parked the plane, lowered the wings, and we unbuckled. I took my time, and as we walked back to the debriefing, parachutes and helmets over our shoulders, Givens smiled and said: "Well, did you feel a bit queasy?"

A Skyraider gropes for *Antietam's* wires off Korea in August 1952. The Korean War spurred production, and by the time the last AD-7, 142081, rolled out in 1957, Douglas had produced 3,180 aircraft — seven main line versions and 28 sub-versions. The Skyraider was nothing if not versatile.

Douglas' firm grip of Navy requirements is clearly shown in this photo — the Douglas Skywarrior, Skyhawk and Skyraider on board *Coral Sea,* May 1963.

(Steve Birdsall)

White smoke streams back from the 20mm cannon as Glenn Givens makes his second pass at a VC hootch line. Givens' plane, BuNo 132582, was built as an AD-5N in the early 1950's. The A-1 is the plane the ground troops like most when they need *real* close air support. *(Steve Birdsall)*

This A-1J, 142016, from 6th Special Operations Squadron, is a recent Navy hand-me-down, here unloading 500-pound bombs. Still on the racks are six frag clusters, making a multi-purpose load. *(USAF)*

AD-5Ws, now EA-1Es, from the *Forrestal*, on duty in April 1960.

2. Fire with Fire

The very first Skyraider, 09085, externally little different from the last. *(Douglas)*

"I AM convinced that the Douglas Skyraider is the best and most effective close support airplane in the world today," said Rear Admiral John M. Hoskins, Commander of Task Force 77 in Korea. "The guts and backbone of the Navy's war in Korea" was another official, more blunt Navy opinion.

VA-55 from the *Valley Forge* was the first squadron to take the AD into action, three days after the Korean War broke out in June 1950. They hit installations around Pyonyang, the capital of North Korea. On Independence Day they destroyed a bridge span and ten locomotives and gunboats. The same month they struck the oil refineries at Wonsan—which blazed for four days.

VA-115 on the *Philippine Sea* joined in to give support to the troops during the Pusan retreat, and was followed by squadrons from *Leyte* and *Boxer*. At the end of the year *Princeton's* VA-159 came to Korea, and in March 1951 the *Bon Homme Richard* and the *Boxer* (this time with VA-702), were added to the list; a list that included most AD units before the half-peace came to Korea.

One of the pilots on board the *Boxer* was John Shone, a reservist flying with VA-702. He said, "Those of us flying the AD felt extremely fortunate in being assigned this type. The planes were extremely stable and dependable, as well as being the most efficient and practical type for the action. In 1950 the jets had not been developed to the

(Left)—Lt. George Everitt in 518 with some of VA-702's ADs. This was one of the units involved with the "Toko-Ri Bridges," novelized by James A. Michener. (Right)—Lt. John Shone from VA-702 sets up for a run on an enemy bridge near Majon-ni, west of Wonsan.

point where they could carry a suitable bomb load or have sufficient endurance to provide close air support for the ground troops. As a result of this deficiency in the newer planes, it was necessary to use the F4U Corsair and the AD to provide close support and to pinpoint bombs to demolish bridges and other small targets in North Korea. The AD, with its 6,000-pound load, had the capability of remaining in the air for six hours. These features were extremely valuable since they permitted the squadron to orbit in front-line positions and be on call at the convenience of ground control.

"At the time we were flying in Korea there was very little that was humorous about our situation, but I still recall when one of our planes made a forced landing at the emergency strip at Kangnung. The next morning Lieutenant Sullivan flew to the field with spare parts and a mechanic, and discovered a bitter battle was being fought in the hills north of the airstrip. In fact the Air Force personnel were beginning to evacuate the place but were waiting for us to get the AD out. The Major in charge invited Sullivan to have some breakfast while he was waiting. He took him to a grass hut with ammunition boxes for tables and chairs, and Sullivan, appalled, could only say, 'Major, if this is the Officer's Club you sure run a sloppy operation here.' Flying from the carriers had all kinds of advantages!

"As far as tactics were concerned, we normally flew in a division of four planes and a minimum of four ADs and four Corsairs on each mission. We very seldom flew high enough to use oxygen because it wasted too much time and fuel to reach those altitudes. When the ADs started a dive bombing run the F4Us would fly along just ahead and strafe any gun positions around the target area. Much of our flying was to provide close air support for the people on the ground.

An AD-6 from VA-16 reflects on its failure to keep on the runway at NAS Oceana, Virginia. November 1957.

A trio of AD-4Bs from VX-5. Rear Admiral Thomas J. Walker, on board *Ticonderoga,* was the first C.O. of this outfit which was developing systems to deliver atomic weapons from carriers using light bombers. Their technique was loft bombing, or over-the-shoulder bombing; the AD would describe a sort of high, graceful script "L", sometimes called an "idiot loop." Admiral Walker smiled, "I was the idiot."

VA-702's pilots on board *Boxer*. John Shone is fourth from the left in the first row.

(John Shone)

Center

Lt. George Everitt from Dallas, a long way from home in a VA-702 AD-2 loaded for bridges near Wonsan.

Bottom

The Royal Navy's Fleet Air Arm called their fifty AD-4W Skyraiders AEW 1s. 778 Squadron at Culdrose, Cornwall, was the first to use them, and one of their aircraft, BuNo 127949, is shown here during the initial training period. Although the aircraft is not as ungainly as she appears, the AD-3Ws and AD-4Ws caused a lot of designers' headaches in the early stages; extensive modifications, like the extra fins, were the result. *(Royal Navy)*

"The AD was an excellent airplane for carrier operations with good response to the controls, even at slow speeds, but I have never seen an airplane with enough spare power to make an 800-foot runway seem long. My greatest concern in Korea was not the enemy guns, but the fear that I would run off the end of the deck before attaining flying speed and drop the plane into the ocean right in front of the carrier. We lost several Corsairs that way, but never an AD, so it was all in my imagination."

As well as all the regular AD equipped squadrons in Korea, the AD-4Ns of VC-35 worked by night with bombs and flares, and the Marines' VMC-1 used AD-4Qs to seek out enemy radar which would then become the target of their bomb-carrying companions, and ADs from *Boxer* even delivered six attacks with explosive-laden F6F Hellcat drones. In Korea the ADs proved themselves. No other aircraft could do what they did. They were the Navy's "Big Gun" in Korea.

Up to now I've told several stories about the Skyraider, but very little about the airplane itself.

The Skyraider was designed for World War II. Douglas' Chief Designer Engineer Ed Heinemann, the man who designed the SBD Dauntless, asked the Navy for time to come up with a replacement for his SBD in 1944. The Navy had requested designs from a couple of other companies, but not Douglas, because they had just cancelled the BTD, that company's intended SBD replacement.

However, the Navy agreed—provided Heinemann could come up with something immediately. So he and two other Douglas designers worked all night in a hotel room and turned in their ideas the following day. The Navy was impressed, and let Douglas into the game, but they had to conform to the schedule set for the two earlier starters.

AD-4NLs from VC-35. Detachments on the carriers off Korea, armed with bombs, flares and searchlights, kept the enemy awake; then the day shift took over.

Left

One of the XBT2D-1s is rotting away in a junk yard on Route 1 in Pennsylvania. It was to be cannibalized for parts for two other XBT2Ds in 1950, but it was in better shape than them, and was spared. For this.

(Bernard Mallon)

Right

One of the Swedish Air Service's twelve bright-yellow target-towing aircraft, purchased from the Royal Navy.

(Lars Lundin)

19

The French got 100 AD-4s from the Navy for use in their Algerian war. This aircraft, 126877, is the second of a batch of 143 AD-4Ns delivered to the USN in 1950. Some of the French ADs were resold to the Cambodian Air Force in 1965, despite U.S. protests, and the VNAF received AD-6s late in 1960. *(Armee de l'Air)*

The XBT2D-1, known as the "Dauntless II," flew for the first time on March 18, 1945, and in May the Navy requested 548 airplanes. It is ironic that those aircraft were being ordered in 1945 to do the job that their descendants would be doing in Vietnam. But the war and the need ended suddenly, and the order was cut to 377, then to 277. In February 1946 they called the plane "Skyraider" and in April the designation changed to "AD-1." Even some of the first twenty-five XBT2Ds were modified for photographic, early warning and night attack or coun-

termeasure roles, unveiling the big eight-and-one-half-ton plane's capabilities.

The AD did not change greatly between World War II and Korea. There was an engine change, increase in fuel load, structural strengthening in the landing gear region, an experiment with a turbo-prop engine and so on, but externally it differed very little prior to its conversion for "other" duties. The big change was in the AD-5, with side-by-side cockpit seating, and the long, large canopy. This was designed as a "basic airframe" with a number of easily

Carrying the big ones, 2000-pounders, one of *Valley Forge's* ADs leaves the rescue helo happily unemployed.

itted modification kits for countermeasures or whatever role was chosen, and is the plane the USAF uses in Vietnam, the A-1E. Modified to carry dual controls, it went into action in June 1964, and it is still there.

In 1965, twenty years after they became operational, A-1s operated with twelve of the fifteen attack carrier air wings. They were officially retired in April 1968, replaced by the Grumman A-6. With the A-6 costing around $4,000,000 and the average A-1 costing $285,000 when in production, the A-6 had better be good. The Air Force

turned to the Skyraider in Vietnam because it was one aircraft with which they could fight the brushfire war with fire. The VNAF A-1 squadrons are converting to jet A-37s, but in the limited battle area that is South Vietnam, the Skyraider still has a place all its own. If the war escalates to the point where MiGs operate south of the DMZ and the whole structure of absolute air supremacy changes, perhaps the A-1 will lose that place. But to this point the Skyraider has kept pace with the intensifications.

SKYRAIDER PRODUCTION

Bureau Number	Model	Bureau Number	Model	Bureau Number	Model	Bureau Number	Model
09085-09019	XBT2D-1	124076-124127	AD-4W	127921-127961	AD-4W	133757-133776	AD-5W
09110-09351	AD-1	124128-125156	AD-4N	128917-129016	AD-4	133854-133929	AD-5
09352-09386	AD-1Q	124725-124760	AD-4N	132227-132391	AD-4B	134466-134637	AD-6
122210-122365	AD-2	124761-124777	AD-4W	132392-132476	AD-5	134974-135054	AD-5N
122366-122387	AD-2Q	125707-125764	AD-4N	132477	AD-5N	135139-135222	AD-5W
122729-122853	AD-3	125765-125782	AD-4W	132478	AD-5	135223-135406	AD-6
122854-122876	AD-3Q	126836-126875	AD-4W	132479	AD-5S	137492-137632	AD-6
122877-122907	AD-3W	126876-127018	AD-4N	132480-132636	AD-5N	139556-139605	AD-5W
122908-122922	AD-3N	127844-127879	AD-4	132637-132686	AD-5	139606-139821	AD-6
123771-124006	AD-4	127880-127920	AD-4N	132729 132792	AD-5W	142010-142081	AD-7
124037-124075	AD-4Q						

While all 3,180 Skyraiders are listed above (in numerical order for ease of reference), a few notes are necessary. A large number of these aircraft were converted, by both Douglas and the Navy. XBT2D-1s were modified for photographic, countermeasures, night attack and early warning roles. Two AD-3Ws became AD-3Es for submarine search, two AD-3Ns the complementary AD-3Ss for submarine attack. AD-4s were winterized for Korea as AD-4L, or modified to AD-4B. AD-4Ns became winterized AD-4NLs, or, stripped for day attack, AD-4NAs. Fifty-four AD-5Ns became AD-5Qs, modified from kits. Several other aircraft were modified as "prototypes" for following versions, etc. The AD-5W and other "W" models are the "Guppies," with the cumbersome bubble beneath the fuselage. A few notes and specifications on the various Skyraiders are also relevant. Up to the AD-4s, armament was two 20mm. wing cannon, then four. Skyraider wing span was 50 feet, length varied between 38'2" on the AD-2 to 40 feet on the AD-5. Empty weight ranged from 10,500 pounds for the XBT2D-1 to 12,600 for the AD-4W, gross from 15,000 to 17,000, and overload from 16,700 to 25,000 for models after the AD-4. Maximum speed was 328 knots in the AD-2, but fell to 260 for the AD-5N and AD-5W; cruising speed in the Skyraider is between 180 and 200 knots. Service ceiling ranged from a low of 25,000 feet for AD-5Ns up to 36,000 feet for the AD-4. The AD-3Ws range from 1,100 nautical miles, the AD-2s 1,386. Crew carried ranged from one in the basic single-seat models, to four in the AD-5Q; up to the AD-5, "Q" aircraft had carried pilot and ECM operator, with access hatch on the right side behind the pilot, and "N" and "W" ADs had carried pilot and two crew, with two access doors and fuselage dive brakes deleted. The best performer, the AD-2, had an initial climb rate of 2,800 feet per minute. All Skyraiders were fitted with the eighteen cylinder Wright R-3350 engine. A final note is that in 1962 the AD-5 became A-1E, AD-5W EA-1E, AD-5Q EA-1F, AD-5N A-1G, AD-6 A-1H and AD-7 A-1J.

Top

One of the 178 AD-2s, cruising over the Japanese Islands while on route to the first war the Skyraider didn't miss—Korea.

Center

Flying gas pump. One of *Intrepid's* ADs refills an F9F photo-recon plane from its 300-gallon centerline tank. The ADs could also be fitted as target two planes, ambulances, mosquito-control spray planes, passenger or cargo carriers, (the 1st Air Commandos in Vietnam have night-dropped food and ammo to ground troops in napalm cans), as well as serving in their main roles: day attack, all-weather attack, electronic countermeasures and airborne early warning.

Bottom

On Sunday, June 20, 1965, she was one of four VA-25 aircraft from USS *Midway* which turned the tables on a MiG-17 near Thanh Hoa. By February 1967 she was flying with VA-52 on board *Ticonderoga,* and on April 10, 1968, back with VA-25, she was at NAS LeMoore for the Navy's A-1 retirement ceremony. Right now she's cocooned, awaiting display facilities in the Naval Air Museum at Pensacola. *(R. T. Maroney, Official USN)*

3. One Man's War

TOM Hansen served on the 37th Air Rescue and Reconnaisance Squadron's HU-16 Albatrosses, the big seaplanes that spent long, lonely hours over the Gulf of Tonkin. They were part of a rescue organization that warmed the heart of every pilot going "north." The HU-16s were accompanied by a variety of A-1s from the carriers on Yankee Station at the time, and Airman Hansen spent a lot of time clicking off pictures of them. They are among the best Skyraider pictures I have ever seen, and I'm grateful to Tom Hansen for the privilege of presenting them.

A couple of *Coral Sea's* Skyraiders slip in close for some pictures during a 1967 Tonkin Gulf patrol.

The wildest A-1 squadron marking of all time, the black and yellow bumblebee of VA-176, on this *Intrepid* A-1J. VA-176 also has a claim to the title of MiG Killers. On October 9, 1966 their MiG was jumped by one trailing A-1 while attacking another. The four 20mm cannon took care of the enemy plane. They also got a "probable."

This bird came from the *Oriskany,* the carrier that suffered a terrible fire that took over forty lives late in 1966.

One of Tico's "Knight Riders." The mean-looking clusters under the wings are 5-inch rockets.

The A-1 pilots were an obliging lot. They were happy to flutter their huge dive brakes and lower the hook and gear—nothing was too much trouble. This bird, from VA-145, "The Swordsmen," wears the Tonkin Gulf Yacht Club badge, a black junk over three red stripes in a yellow circle.

Hancock's main claim to fame was probably the nimble three-toed maintenance man who left his mark on this A-1, nominally assigned to Lt. Commander Jack Jones.

First Air Commando Spad, loaded down with a dozen reasons why our ground troops love the A-1s. This machine carries four small napalm cans and eight CBUs, the kind of ordnance the Pleiku pilots like best. *(USAF)*

4. Bloody Valley at A Shau

(Left)—Probably both lucky to be alive, Bernie Fisher and Jump Myers at Pleiku. Fisher, now a Lt. Colonel flying F-106s, has this to say: "I'm sure there are greater powers than we who guide us so tenderly in time of need ... that force which bridges the gap and allows us to succeed where otherwise we must fail. I'm grateful for many things, not the least of them those comrades who were so capable and reliable when the need was greatest." (Right)—Carrying everything but a turkey dinner for the North Koreans, one of Bonny Dick's ADs takes off for a Thanksgiving Day strike, 1952.

THERE was, over the bar at the airconditioned officers' club at Pleiku, an unframed portrait of a shyly smiling, sandy-haired pilot. His name was Major Bernard (Bernie) Fisher of the 1st Air Commando Squadron.

Bernie Fisher, a 39-year-old Mormon from Idaho, did not swear, smoke or drink liquor; he stuck to milk. And yet he was at home in this bar where all three vices were rife. No problem. Fisher found his excitement elsewhere; in October 1965 he had won the D.F.C. after locating a shot-down airman and giving him covering fire until a chopper picked him up.

The First Air Commandos were professionals—most had flown the hottest jet fighters. Their average age was thirty-eight, most were majors. All had flown tight missions, yet all were one in their admiration of Bernie Fisher. Fisher won the Congressional Medal of Honor for what he did on March 10, 1966.

The Special Forces camp at A Shau, forty miles from Da Nang, is in a mountain valley just a few miles from the Laotian border. Held by 17 American Green Berets, 140 mercenaries and 250 Vietnamese irregulars, the still uncompleted camp awoke to the clinking of North Vietnamese shovels on March 9, as the enemy dug trenches below the south wall of the triangular fortress. About 4 A.M. mortars began exploding, kept hitting all over the camp—three a minute—in a barrage that lasted all day. At dawn the first enemy troops attacked but were cut down and forced to pull out.

A Shau was locked in. The clouds, thick and moist, rose from 200 feet above the valley up to 8,000 feet. Air support, our iron fist, was locked out.

Early that morning an AC-47 Dragon Ship, armed with 6,000 round-per-minute mini-guns, got through the ceiling. Before its guns were fired the potent DC-3 went down about two miles from the camp. Three of the crew were killed fighting from the wreckage of their plane. Then two HH-43 Huskies from Da Nang felt their way through the clouds, and while one gave covering fire the other picked up the gunship's crew. The three wounded men ran to Captain Andy Solberg's chopper and the crew pulled them aboard, firing back at the enemy. Then two men from the second chopper went looking for the rest of the AC-47 crew. In the wrecked aircraft they found two dead. All six had survived the crash landing, now three were wounded (one critically), two were dead, and one missing, presumed dead.

Flying out of Thailand and South Vietnam, Air Force A-1s, known for the mission as "Sandys," perform perhaps their most rewarding task, escorting rescue choppers plucking downed pilots from the enemy's lair. *(USAF)*

132649, the plane Bernie Fisher landed at A Shau, returns with empty racks from an earlier mission. She has just unloaded 7,000 pounds of bombs on a Viet Cong tunnel complex in the bitterly contested "Zone D," capping the job by strafing the occupants. *(USAF)*

At Pleiku, Bernie Fisher had been briefed for an out-of-country mission when he was diverted to A Shau. When Fisher arrived, he found a bunch of planes droning over the thick cloud, looking for a hole. He managed to find one. The big, soot-stained Skyraider rolled down and white smoke poured back across the wings from the four cannons as Fisher began his strafing pass. He went back soon after to bring down friends.

An old Huey helicopter and two more groups of A-1s got through, a couple of C-123s dropped supplies, and two B-57 Canberras brought down rockets and napalm.

At 6 A.M. on March 10, Fisher received word he was being recommended for the Silver Star. The next few hours were to change all that.

At 10:15 A.M. the co-ordinates that translated as A Shau crackled over the radio, and Fisher and his wingman changed course from their scheduled strike. Again, other planes were looking for a way through the clouds that smothered A Shau—four other A-1Es, two from the 602nd Fighter Squadron based near Qui Nhon.

The Korean War was almost over when *Lake Champlain* reached Korean waters, but her ADs managed to get

Fisher again took the lead; two planes stayed in reserve, north of the fortress, while he took the other three six miles down the valley—a valley less than a mile across and heavily defended by North Vietnamese guns.

In the camp itself, the Vietnamese irregulars, feeling the time had come to reassess the situation, called off an assault on the south wall, joined the North Vietnamese, and turned their fire on the other defenders. This lost the south wall and the Americans called in Fisher and his followers to hit the wall with everything they had.

Fisher was followed by his wingman, Captain Paco Vazquez, and Major Dafford W. Myers of the 602nd, with his wingman, Captain Hub King.

King was hit first. A burst of machine gun fire shattered his canopy and missed him by inches. Unable to see through the cracked glass, King climbed out of the valley.

"Jump" Myers had just completed a strafing pass, when he felt his aircraft shudder. His engine coughed and started stalling, then died. The cockpit was choked by smoke. He radioed: "I've been hit. Hit hard."

their bombs dropped—501 has 18 missions, 515 has 13, as does 503.

Fisher could see Myers' plane was burning right along the fuselage. The only chance for Myers, too low to bail out, was to land on the steel mat strip below, then try to get to the camp.

Myers was blinded by the smoke in the cockpit, but Fisher talked him in. The rest was mostly Myers' intuition. He jettisoned the last of his ordnance, but his centerline auxiliary tank was hung up and would not drop. He went in, listening to Fisher's terse corrections. At the last minute Fisher burst out: "You're too hot! Get your gear up. You'll have to belly her in."

Myers hit the runway while his landing gear was still retracting. It was mangled. The gas tank exploded beneath the Skyraider in a sheet of flame, and the plane careened down the runway, lurched to the right and crashed into the embankment along the edge of the 2,500-foot strip.

As Myers opened the sliding side window of the plane, the flames poured in. He knew to get through the flames he'd have to leave his survival vest and dive through the right window. Although he was in the fiercely burning wreck for a full minute, he managed to act without panic. The window opened and a strong and benevolent wind down the runway opened a path through the flames, to a friendly clump of weeds.

Fisher, surprised Myers was alive, called for a rescue chopper, but it would have taken at least fifteen minutes. The main thing at the moment was to cover Myers with everything the A-1Es had. He could see enemy soldiers on the embankment separating Myers from the fort. He put three 100-pound bombs on them, came around and put four more on the opposite side of the runway. In doing so he took hits from the east ridge, so Vazquez, following him, went and plastered it.

It was then that Fisher decided he was going to land and pick Myers up. He called in the two First Air Commandos A-1Es, farther up the valley, for fire support. With Vazquez, Captains John Lucas and Dennis Hague, Hobo 27 and 28, hosed the place down with cannon fire,

Fisher's Shau aircraft was landed on a short emergency strip with a smoking engine on a later mission. Realizing he would overshoot the runway, the pilot jerked the gear up, and the ship caught fire. Rescued by a "Flying Crane," she's now with the Air Force Museum at Wright-Patterson AFB. That bent-up prop is a memorial at Pleiku. *(USAF)*

In May 1957 this AD-5N took off from *Forrestal,* struck fuel trouble, and crash-landed near Ranes, France.
(Maurice Salbert)

Deck crewmen weave in and out, getting ADs set up for take-off from *Midway* during the February 1954 NATO Operation, Turkish Sky I.

An AD-5W falls off the end of the deck, the crew unbuckles, then stands up to receive rescue chopper. Carrier pilots all fear a "cold shot," being cat-launched without sufficient power.

This is the aircraft in which Major Bernard Fisher did the impossible. Completely restored and repainted by the Air Force Museum at Wright Patterson, she is the sole surviving "Medal of Honor aircraft."
(Air Force Museum)

A VA-145 bird skims along *Essex's* deck a split second before piling up.

illing an estimated company of North Vietnamese forming up to charge the camp's east wall. The Special Forces troops, the twelve who survived, considered that this attack was what saved them, and gave them time to pull out.

The runway looked bad—Myers' wrecked A-1E, gasoline drums, jagged spears of PSP runway, rocket pods—debris everywhere.

Fisher's first landing attempt was fouled up by a cloud of smoke that passed across the runway and enveloped his plane. Next time he got her down, he raised the flaps and jabbed the brakes before the tailwheel touched the ground. He steered around the mortar holes as the end of the runway got closer. He couldn't risk slamming the brakes for fear of nosing over, so he let the big fighter roll off the strip onto the grass, then hit the left brake and slewed the aircraft right around. He drove up the runway to where Myers was waving from the grass, believing his benefactor had shared his fate.

Expended shells and belt links from the three Skyraiders

strafing fifty feet above, showered Myers. One of the three aircraft, Lucas', hit badly, was on fire. On the last pass all three were out of ammunition, but the dry run was enough to keep the enemy troops' heads down.

Myers suddenly realized what was happening. Crouching as low as he could, and running as fast as he could, he sprinted 200 yards down the center of the open runway.

He grabbed a handhold on the fuselage of the aircraft, stumbled across the wing, and dived head first into the cockpit. Perforated by nineteen hits, Fisher's plane still ran smoothly as they roared from the runway and left A Shau behind.

Myers, without a headset, couldn't talk to Fisher. He sat in the cockpit, red eyed from the smoke, his scorched clothes caked with mud. He conveyed to Fisher by sign language that he could use a cigarette, but of course Fisher couldn't help. Myers just looked at him and gave him a couple of hugs. Then they started laughing.

Lt. Bui Dinh Giang walked away from this belly-landing at Bien Hoa in June 1966. His aircraft had taken hits from groundfire during a close air support mission. *(USAF)*

5. Four Years to Die

Major Lester Hewitt, American Advisor at Da Nang.

TRAVELING around South Vietnam you heard a lot opinions about the VNAF pilots. These ran the full gam from good to bad. But perhaps the most valid came fro somebody who flew with them.

At Da Nang I talked with Major Lester R. Hewitt, American advisor with AFAT-5. He had had 600 hours A-1s. This is what he told me: "I rate the Vietnamese good as anybody else as pilots—their ability reflects the training." I asked him what kind of missions they fle from Da Nang? He replied, "mostly ground support rol —direct air support or close air support, convoy escort."

I heard about one of Da Nang's VNAF pilots, Capta Thai Van De, of the 516th Fighter Squadron. He had wo the Silver Star for his part in the A Shau battle on Mar 9, 1966. On that day Major Hewitt was his wingman.

"Captain De came over in the morning expecting an Shau mission. They didn't expect it to hold out. All tl Army brass were worried and they had orders from Wes moreland to hold the airstrip. The last report was that tl south wall had been taken and they were just holding on a couple of bunkers on the inside and the two other wall We knew which wall we could hit and that the weath was terrible.

Bad news for the Viet Cong. This VNAF A-1E, carrying student pilot and American instructor, is loaded up with twelve seven-rocket pods to deconcentrate a VC troop concentration. *(USAF)*

VNAF A-1Es fold their wings as they return from a strike in South Vietnam. *(USAF)*

The VNAF flight line at Da Nang. The third ship was bellied in, and stands engineless behind the Award of the Mangled Propeller. *(Tom Hansen)*

"The Vietnamese fighter pilot lives for four years . . . most of the pilots in my squadron will be dead in 1970. We come over here as tigers for a year. It's not fear with the VNAF, it's the stacked odds.

"Anyway, I called De aside and told him, 'If anything happens to you I'll take care of your family.'

"We scrambled a little past noon and were airborne in less than fifteen minutes. As we neared the outpost we saw that it was completely blanketed by clouds, so we headed north and found a hole to drop through. De didn't have the right ordnance. We had 100-pound white phosphorus and 250-pound frags—I would've liked napalm. As I said, there was this hole—sort've—you would barely see part of the airfield. Down De goes through the hole and I follow him. I didn't know what the hell was going on. De headed south, we crossed a ridge, made a left turn and

boy, there was the camp. There was a lot of ground fire and explosions. We didn't know it, but we were the first A-1s there . . . first aircraft was an AC-47. There were two layers of cloud and we were below safe operating level. We came in and the guys on the ground marked the target for us with white phosphorus. We dropped level, putting it pretty good—right in there—and blanketed the place. An Army Caribou that we'd seen circling above the cloud had followed us down the hole. We had terrible radios then and he was coming down the valley and through the pass at 100 feet. I called De and he didn't drop his bombs because of the Caribou. The transport dropped by parachute and got out. We expended our bombs, then we started with 20 mm. De was hit pretty bad—no hydraulic power so he couldn't charge his guns. We went back up through the hole. The VNAF got no credit.

"De and I went back next day. That was when Fisher came in. We saw the crashed A-1 and we knew something was going on. We were lobbing our bombs trying to scare some of the fifty caliber they had in the hills around there." Hewitt paused a moment, shook his head: "That was kinda classic, just the situation."

Hewitt got back to talking about the airplanes: "I don't think there's anything to compare to it. A little heavy for this kind of warfare. The P-47—you know, the old Thunderbolt—might be better. But it's a terrific airplane. You feel good as a pilot flying it because you've got all that armor plating. We don't need beefed up landing gear—if you land and need a lot of brakes you've screwed up somewhere else." [Some A-1E pilots had said the brakes, designed for carrier use, weren't as good as they could be.] "You can't lock the brakes. It's real fine. The cockpit's

too small for the size of the airplane, but the Vietnamese are too small for the cockpit—they pile up newspapers and all sorts of things just so they can get up high enough on the seats and reach the pedals. The A-1H is better than the E or J—better visibility mainly, and a little better performance. The guns are real good, you don't have to harmonize them all the time. You can get as good a pattern of fire from 2,000 to 2,400 as pressing it right in. We dive bomb at 1,500 to 1,100 feet, and at a 1,000 feet we level bomb. It's real accurate—just forget about the gunsight. It's slow but after a while you get tremendous accuracy—in a jet you couldn't hope to do this."

Hewitt, a volunteer as all VNAF advisors are, sums up the VNAF and Captain De: "I couldn't ask for a finer pilot to fly with."

Mission completed, Da Nang. *(Tom Hansen)*

Carrying a light bomb load, an A-1 from the 516th Squadron at Da Nang taxies out from the line for takeoff. *(Tom Hansen)*

A VNAF A-1H at Da Nang. It was photographed from behind a grassy anti-blast wall to get a shot of the crew working on the ship. Once the Vietnamese see a camera pointed in their direction they usually smile and pose.
(Steve Birdsall)

Previously with Nguyen Cao Ky's old outfit, 83rd Special Operations at Tan Son Nhut, this aircraft carried UL tail code, symbolic cowl marking, and the 83rd's own dragon insignia on the fuselage. Here, with the 516th Squadron, she is partially repainted. The VNAF use these fuselage bands for identification—at Da Nang white stars on blue, at Bien Hoa black and yellow checks, at Pleiku white arrows on a red band.

I wanted to see the VNAF in action, and the best way to get good pictures and watch them at work is from an O-1E FACing for them. It looked like a good mission. One of Bien Hoa's FACs, Major Howe, who also respects the VNAF A-1 pilots, had requested a strike on a very obstinate target, a bridge that had been cut but quickly repaired, and could be again as long as the spans remained

intact. The FAC wanted a couple of VNAF A-1s with 2,000-pound bombs to take out those spans.

But TACC, the Tactical Air Control Center in Saigon, had not approved it. The FAC was apologetic as we sipped hot chocolate in his air-conditioned trailer early that morning. I told him not to feel bad, war is hell. He looked hurt and said: "It ain't much, but it's all we've got."

A Skyraider on *Ranger* fires up while deck crewmen take a breather.

6. The Tonkin Gulf Yacht Club

FIFTEEN minutes from U.S.S. *Ticonderoga's* position on Yankee Station, a couple of hundred miles from Da Nang, I put on my orange survival vest and strapped in. As the minutes passed I watched through the little window at my side, straining in the harness to see the ship. The water started to come up, then suddenly, momentarily, the deck flashed by—planes, men in colored jackets, gray superstructure. The wheels touched, the hook caught the wire, the pilot gunned the engines. Then we were taxiing forward. Landing on a carrier facing backwards is a memorable experience.

U.S.S. *Ticonderoga* is one of the older carriers operating in Vietnam. She had been on Dixie Station, supporting allied operations in the Mekong Delta, and now her pilots had graduated to the bigger league—Yankee Station. An *Essex* class carrier, her keel was laid in February 1943 and on January 21, 1945 a Japanese kamikaze screamed into the deck. Burning, "Tico" became her own target marker as smoke billowed from her stricken decks. Her gunners knocked down three attackers, but another suicide plane broke through the barrage, slammed into the ship and started fierce fires. So *Ticonderoga* is an old warrior, well scarred.

Commander Robert R. Worchesek and aircraft 311, (previously 384), at Tay Ninh.

How soon will the Skyraider be a thing of the past? The USAF seems firmly committed to using it in Vietnam until the end. There are several A-1s memorialized around the world; the Aircraft Industries Museum in Kentucky has an AD-5, Royal Naval Air Station Culdrose has two FAA Skyraiders, WT121 and WV106, and probably the most unique memorabilia is the San Diego Aero Space Museum's complete set of Lt. Dieter Dengler's underwear, along with his clothes, worn by Dengler as a prisoner of the Pathet Lao and North Vietnamese.

(Tom Hansen)

Lt. Commander Bill McGrath straps into 311 as the crew put the finishing touches to their work. *(Steve Birdsall)*

Flashback. January 21, 1945, and Tico reels under kamikaze attacks near Formosa.

Ticonderoga, a World War II vintage *Essex* Class carrier twice kamikazed in 1945, steams placidly through the South China Sea.

My first stop on Tico was Ready Five, Attack Squadron 52's briefing room. Their CO was Commander Robert R. Worchesek, and I had already met him at Operations at Da Nang. His A-1 had followed our COD out from the line, so he was already back. Worchesek was an A-1 pilot from way back, so I decided to ask him some questions. His first A-1 flight was back in January 1950, a training flight in an AD-1 at Corpus Christi. He'd flown with VA-15 at NAS Jacksonville, VA-45 in the Mediterranean and Korea, then ATU-307 at Corpus Christi in the AD-1, AD-2, AD-3 and AD-4 as an instructor. Then he went to VA-44 and VA-176 at Jacksonville, VA-122 at LeMoore, and finally VA-52 in November 1965. He had racked up 3,500 hours in A-1s, and flown each and every model.

As a man vastly qualified to speak about the Skyraider, he said: "The main fault of the A-1 is its low speed in this highly modern environment." I asked about its greatest virtues. "A couple—one is time on station, next ability to carry a very heavy load, next its versatility. Not only a heavy load, but anything you *want*. It's an excellent weapons platform. The A-1Hs and A-1Js aren't vastly superior to the AD-1. There have been a lot of improvements over the years—the finest was the AD-2. It was the fastest. First of the modern versions."

I asked Commander Worchesek what his most memorable Skyraider experience was: "I ditched one once after the throttle linkage broke, and in 1951 I had the Atlantic Fleet record for dive bombing in AD-1s—I had a competitive average of 21 feet for six bombs. Of course my biggest one was at Tay Ninh."

When I went aboard I'd first met the squadron's XO, Commander Paul Merchant. He was an experienced A-1 pilot but he would much rather fly jets. He told me to talk to the CO . . . "He likes the A-1 because I don't think he's ever flown anything else." In Commander Merchant's opinion the A-1 has outlived its usefulness here on Yankee Station. I asked Worchesek if he agreed: "Yes," he said, "but I think we're going to miss the A-1. Particularly for the in-country work. It could do just an outstanding job . . . that jets can't do."

During Tico's last cruise, down south on Dixie Station, Worchesek was in aircraft 311. He told me the following story: "I was on a bombing run in 311, and after the fact it appears the top rudder hinge bracket broke as I pulled out. The top half of the rudder folded completely over . . . there was a hole in the top where it hit the tail hook. When the rudder broke the areodynamic forces pulled the stick back—I was in a forty degree dive at 350 knots. Because of the stick being pulled back, both outboard elevator hinges were taken out and both elevators bent straight down from the inner hinge position . . . both dragged on the ground on landing. I wasn't able to get enough forward stick to keep the nose down, so I had to roll over on my back, allow the nose to drop, get below the horizon, roll out, get the nose up, roll over and so on until I found a place to put her down. The wheels and flaps slowed it down, but even on final I had problems."

After spiraling along for a while Worchesek was able to land at Tay Ninh, which was unsecured at the time. So a Marine guard stood watch over the aircraft all night, and next day a Sikorsky Flying Crane lifted her out. Unfortunately when they put old 311 down again at Da Nang they dropped her from about six feet up. Somehow 311 had survived all this, and she looked good—but flew sideways.

Skyraiders hold the record for single-engine load hauling—14,940 pounds useful load, 3,000 pounds more than their own empty weight!

This photo of a VA-52 practice run was pinned to a notice board near Tico's Wardroom. Caption was: "This Navy-Air Force sortie race is getting ridiculous!" *(Douglas)*

The afternoon was only half over, so one of the pilots took me up to Vulture's Row on the carrier's island to watch a recovery. All around the ship there were planes circling. A rescue helo was on station, and the deck crewmen in their bright jackets were waiting. Most of them were young, and their jobs were dangerous. My escort, Lieutenant Gene Dehnert, told me how they became a little blasé, every now and then about their jobs. He told me about the unfortunate crewman who thought it was a little time-wasting to walk back and behind the blast from a Crusader's engine—he decided to jump over it. He was blown a hundred feet along the deck and spent the next two weeks in hospital.

Then the first Crusader was in the groove. The deck wires were taut as the giant airplane rocketed toward us. It slammed to the deck, caught the fourth wire and moved

MiG Killers. Lt. C. B. Johnson from *Midway's* VA-25 was in 577 on Sunday, June 20, 1965, when four of squadron's planes got a MiG-17 about fifty miles from Thanh Hoa. On RESCAP, the A-1s jumped two MiG They dived to treetop level after jettisoning their fuel and bombs, leveled off and set up the Thach Weave fensive pattern, enabling each pair to protect each other's tails. After trying to get at them for a while, one of Migs headed for home, but the other lined up on the planes flown by LCDR Greathouse and Lt. (j.g.) Lynne, and 571. They turned, and the MiG followed, passing in front of Lt. Hartman in 573 and Johnson in 577. Th opened up with a broadside that set the Red plane afire. It nosed down into a ridge 700 feet below. Johns and Hartman each got the Silver Star and a half kill. Just visible on the scoreboard below the canopy is silhouette of that MiG.

on up the deck to be spotted. More Crusaders came in, followed by Douglas Skyhawks, then Skyraiders, and the recovery was completed. It was the end of the day for Tico. Their pilots and planes usually didn't fly at night. The largest and most modern carrier on Yankee Station at the time, U.S.S. *Kitty Hawk,* equipped with the new, sophisticated all-weather A-6 Intruders and 1,700 m.p.h. Phantoms, took care of that.

The ship was quiet, and as the day faded we walked across the wide deck. The wind made my clothes flap and the deck, greasy and thick with graphite, was unnervingly unsteady beneath my feet. The graphite came from the arresting wires. Made of steel, they must be constantly greased to cut down the fantastic amount of friction when a plane like the Crusader hangs on them, and the grease is splattered all over the deck. By the Landing Signal

One of VA-215's A1s moves up past Sidewinder equipped F-8s, soon to head out on a flak suppression mission.

Navy A-1s have been fighting in Vietnam since August 1964, but now they have finally left the inventory, their squadrons converting to Grumman A-6s. VA-215's losses over the North during this time were among the reasons.

Officer's platform a deck crewman lay reading a book, and a few men worked on the aircraft silhouetted nearby.

I was bunked with two of VA-52's pilots, Lieutenant (j.g.) John Lee and Ensign Cal Van Dorn. My bunk had been vacant since December 1966 when Lieutenant William Natter, from Attack 52, had been shot down. Hit aft, Natter's A-1 had no aileron or rudder control. He was at about 100 feet, and the plane caught fire. He ditched right off Hon Met, just north of Vinh, and was pulled out by a Navy chopper. He lived to read in a Chinese newspaper about how he went to his doom in a ball of flame. The Playboy calendar and "Family Album" above the bunk were mute testimony to his hurried departure.

The next morning I made my way down to the Wardroom for breakfast. I found the Navy can treat you well. Orange juice, coffee, toast, eggs, bacon—quite a change from the garbage truck at Tan Son Nhut. First on the agenda was Snoopy's battle with the Red Baron in the ship's newspaper, the "Tiger Times." Then the conversation turned to less important things. Knowing my interest in the old Skyraider, VA-52 treated me like one of the family. This squadron, the "Knight Riders," was created in February 1959, and was first deployed on Tico in March 1960. At the end of 1961 they'd flown 13,500 accident free hours and were awarded the 1961 Pacific Fleet Battle Efficiency Pennant. They deployed aboard

One of the first batch of the 713 AD-6 Skyraiders, here with VA-152. A detachment from this squadron was selected to be sent to Tan Son Nhut to train VNAF A-1 pilots.

U.S.S. *Lexington* for a cruise around Cape Horn and made history when six of their Skyraiders were launched and recovered during the usual violent weather and boiling seas around the Horn. In April 1964 they were back on board *Ticonderoga,* and on August 2 they were scrambled to repel North Vietnamese PT boats attacking a U.S. destroyer in a historic "incident." On the fourth and fifth of August they flew retaliatory strikes against North Vietnam, as part of Air Wing Five. In September 1965 they embarked on Tico for a second Vietnam cruise and from November 1965 to May 1966 flew over 1,500 day and night close air support sorties. Then in May 1966 they returned to NAS Alameda and became part of Air Wing Nineteen.

Due to the official ruling I could not fly with VA-52, because they don't fly scheduled in-country missions. So I spent most of my time in the comparative luxury of the Ready Room, watching replays of landings on closed-circuit television, listening in on the briefings and generally learning what I could about the men and planes. And I listened to stories. One of the best stories concerned a pilot they called "Spad" Wilson. He really can do things with the A-1 I was told, and from the landing record board —a square for each landing made alongside the name of the pilot and filled in with a different color for each kind of landing—OK, fair, or dangerous—it appeared that was correct. Anyway, at one time VA-52's pilots had sent for a number of profiles on the A-1, but some idiot had sent

While two A-1s that are going out are being refueled, re-armed and checked out, the forward deck has to be cleared. This just-returned A-1 is 300, specially

marked "CAG's aircraft," although the Air Wing Commander, CDR Billy Phillips, preferred 400, his F-8, or 500, his A-4 Skyhawk.

(Left)—The tail tip and upper and lower stripes are blue, and within them, separated by neutral strips, a thicker yellow bar is outlined by two red stripes. These markings also border the fuselage band. Lettering along fuselage reads: COMATKCARAIRWING NINETEEN. (Right)—306 is about to join 311 on a late afternoon mission. The plane is just back from the Philippines and a re-paint job, and the mace hasn't been added to the "Knight Rider's" blue band.

Aircraft 311 has just landed and is going right out again. As the plane is fueled, other crewmen check tire wear and prepare to fit new belts of twenty millimeter. *(Steve Birdsall)*

them about a hundred copies of the story of the Bristol Bulldog. So on the next mission Wilson radioed to flight control, "Four Bristol Bulldogs ready for takeoff." The new name didn't take on like "Spad," but it still came up occasionally.

When pulled out of the attacks on the flak-infested strategic areas of the North, and North Vietnam and various other dangerous maneuvers, another pilot told of A-1s searching for sharks on the shallow reefs and shooting them up with 20 mm. just to pass the time.

Now after all those years the A-1s are out of the Navy, but at that time they were being used for Sea Dragon missions—coastal interdiction, RESCAP—flying escort for patrolling Air Force HU-16s and other rescue aircraft over the Gulf of Tonkin, and Steel Tiger missions. They still got into some hot situations duelling with coastal batteries. On board Tico was Skyraider BuNo 135300, which had been with the *Midway* "MiG Killers," and at one time BuNo 142081, the last Skyraider built, had been there. Most of VA-52's pilots had a plane which carried their name below the cockpit, but they didn't necessarily fly in it. BuNo 142081 had been Lieutenant Steve McBride's

and he was still broken up, at the time, about the fact that Lieutenant Jim Donohue had caught some ground fire nineteen miles west of Bien Hoa. "That was the only plane I've ever had my name on," he confided sadly. We surmised that 142081 probably became the spare parts department of the Cambodian Air Force. Another pilot summed up yet another school of thought: "We ought to say to the North Vietnamese, you blow up a bridge, we'll push a plane over the side."

My first call of the day was Primary Flight Control—"Pri-Fly." From behind its green tinted windows the Air Boss controlled the launch and recovery operations. Again I watched the planes arriving, but this time with narration. The operation went smoothly except for a couple of "bolters," aircraft that missed the wires and zoomed across the deck and into the air again for another try. But so many things could go wrong—all landings were replayed on television in the ready rooms for the pilots' benefit. Sitting in Ready Five I watched a Skyraider flown by Commander Worchesek fly in, catch the wire, and drop a Zuni rocket from under the wing. The rocket zipped along the deck and over the side to a jolly chorus of

One of *Ticonderoga's* Skyraiders moves into line to be catapulted. Dixie Station, April 1964.

One of VAW-13's EA-1Fs, previously AD-5Q, at Da Nang. The EA-1Fs still serve in the Navy's counter-measure squadrons. Lt. Hollis Harmon, still flying them with VAQ-33 on *Intrepid,* insists they have to "convince them that they can still fly." Consistent reminder of the age of their aircraft is the sprinkling of midnight-blue replacement parts that still come through. Navy aircraft have been painted gray since the mid-1950's. *(Tom Hansen)*

LCDR Lawrence Brumbaugh scrambles aboard a VA-52 A-1H on USS *Ticonderoga.* Target: V. C.

Stopping over at Da Nang is "Puff the Magic Dragon" from the aged *Intrepid*. Pilot LCDR Speed Ritzmann chose the name after some very successful night armed-recon missions. Also along were 210, "Shush Boomer," and 203, "The Gloppitta Glopita Machine." *(Tom Hansen)*

"There goes a Zuni, there goes a Zuni." A faulty bracket I guessed, evidently nothing new. Somebody said that on the last cruise they almost decided to perfunctorily sound General Quarters before the A-1s landed. But to me it seemed death and injury were very close to the men flying from, and working on, carriers, and they took their job with the seriousness that it deserved.

The place to feel a carrier's pulse is the Flight Deck, so I requisitioned a red-zippered jacket with "VA-52 Ordnance Officer" on the back of it and a pair of red "Mickey Mouse" ears—sound deadeners on a cloth cap—and went up on deck, fully conscious that if my disguise caused someone to believe I was a working crewman this could be the worst carrier disaster since Midway.

The planes that would be going out were being fired up and the deck was alive with their sound and the heat waves streamed from their jet engines. Deck crewmen were ducking in and out around the jets, working swiftly. Everything about a launch or recovery was done swiftly and precisely by men who were at work for up to eighteen hours a day. Between launches they found something to do—read, sleep maybe, or play Simon and Garfunkel records. Standing close to a giant twin-engined Skywarrior the heat was so great that sweat poured down my face. The engines made the deck windier and more turbulent than ever. But soon they were gone, and more were ready to return.

We walked over to the Landing Signal Officer's platform. The LSO was Lieutenant Chuck Mattraw, one of

LCDR Leisy in 307 will take off second on this seven plane "Steel Tiger" mission against truck parks on the Ho Chi Minh Trail in Laos. Following him is 302, then, Lt. (j.g.) George Duskin in 310, LCDR Bob Reynolds in 309, Lt. (j.g.) Gene Dehnert in 303 and Lt. Jules Gustie in 304. Although they will hit the trucks, Reynolds will have the most exciting trip when his rubber donut bursts beneath him on the pull-out from a dive.

Commander John F. Wanamaker, an AD pilot in the Korean War and VA-52 Operations Officer, moves up to the catapult in 300.

VA-165 Spad ready to go on *Intrepid.* In 1966 she became an all-attack carrier, with two Skyhawk squadrons on board, and two A-1 outfits, VA-165 and VA-176.

VA-52's pilots. Landings were no longer controlled by a man with colored signal flags. Automation in the form of the "mirror," with its colored lights, had taken over. Now the LSO's job was to check out landing visually, and rate them. Mattraw took me over to the very end of the carrier deck and showed me the dents in the metal where aircraft just hadn't made it. I was told that if the other three men on the platform suddenly dived into the safety net below it, I was to do likewise, but there were no shot up aircraft coming in so it probably wouldn't be necessary. As we looked down into the swirling, pale green wake Mattraw told me how he had seen A-1s just torque roll right into it. Power is crucial, too much and not enough are both dangerous.

The four Skyraiders coming in were ready, and the recovery began. First was 300, then John Lee in 311. Both came in well, their wheels and tailhooks looking awkward as the big planes hung on their props and slammed into

Commander Paul G. Merchant, VA-52's Exec, in 302. His instructions during the briefing: "If you get into trouble and have to land in Laos, don't."
(Steve Birdsall)

305 comes aboard *Ticonderoga*. This aircraft, BuNo 135300, reassigned, was one of *Midway's* MiG killers.

A couple of Bonny Dick's A-1s stop in at Da Nang, where there is a very fine Officer's Club. *(Tom Hansen)*

the deck, but the third seemed to hang in the air a little more, and mush down like a brick. "Sonuvabitch"! Mattraw exploded. He turned to the man at his side who kept the landing ratings in a notebook and said: "Not enough power—and put a box around it."

The recovery completed, we moved forward to where aircraft 311, one of the four that had just landed, was being readied for another flight. The aircraft was swarming with deck crewmen in red, yellow, purple, brown and green jackets. Aircraft 306 was nearby, already prepared.

Up forward the catapult was being cleared. A Crusader was going down on the elevator, the three other Skyraiders that had just come aboard were spotted, one behind the other, close to the side of the ship.

Minutes passed, then the Skyraider's engine started and the plane edged forward to the catapult. The cat crew scurried around, rigging up the sling. The signal came, the plane roared forward in a cloud of steam, groped for height at the end of the deck and headed out across the water. VA-52 was in business again.

VA-52 AIRCRAFT COMPLEMENT, JANUARY 1967

300	BuNo	134569	304	BuNo	134515	308	BuNo	139634
301	BuNo	135332	305	BuNo	135300	309	BuNo	137559
302	BuNo	134570	306	BuNo	134577	310	BuNo	135243
303	BuNo	135336	307	BuNo	134614	311	BuNo	142023

THE ARCO-AIRCAM AVIATION SERIES
The first pictorial survey of famous aircraft

Each title illustrates one type or major sub-type of a famous aircraft in the color schemes and markings of the Air Forces of the World. Each contains an **eight-page, four-color insert illustrating 48 planes with all their markings in full color;** supporting black-and-white plan view drawings showing both upper and under surfaces; 125 half-tone photographs, many never before published, of the aircraft in action; plus full-color illustrations showing twenty examples of Unit Insignia of the World's Air Forces. Complete technical specifications including dimensions, weights, performance, power unit, armament, and price are provided for each plane, along with a concise history of their roles in both peace and war time.

Each title: 7¼″ x 9¾″; full-color illustrations

LR cloth: $5.00 ; Paper: $2.95

No. 1–NORTH AMERICAN P-51D MUSTANG
No. 2–REPUBLIC P-47 THUNDERBOLT
No. 3–NORTH AMERICAN MUSTANG MK. I-IV
No. 4–SUPERMARINE SPITFIRE MK. I-XVI, Merline Engine
No. 5–NORTH AMERICAN P-51 B/C MUSTANG
No. 6–CURTISS KITTYHAWK MK. I-IV
No. 7–CURTISS P-40D-N WARHAWK
No. 8–SUPERMARINE SPITFIRE MK. XII-24; SUPERMARINE SEAFIRE MK. 1-47
No. 9–SPAD SCOUTS SVII-SXIII
No. 10–LOCKHEED P-38 LIGHTNING
No. 11–CONSOLIDATED B-24-M LIBERATOR
No. 12–AVRO LANCASTER
No. 13–BATTLE OF BRITAIN
No. 14–THE FINNISH AIR FORCE, 1918-1968

No. 15–NAKAJIMA Ki. 43, HAYABUSA I-III
No. 16–REPUBLIC F/RF-84F THUNDERFLASH/ THUNDERSTREAK
No. 17–BOEING B-17 FLYING FORTRESS N 44
No. 18–MITSUBISHI ABM-ZERO-SEN
No. 19–NORTH AMERICAN F-86A-H SABRE. Volume I
No. 20–NAKAJIMA Ki. 27
No. 21–SHARKMOUTH, Volume I
No. 22–SHARKMOUTH, Volume II
No. 23–CZECH AIR FORCE, 1914-1969
No. 24–GRUMMAN F6F - HELLCAT
No. 25–NORTH AMERICAN F-86A, Volume II
No. 26–KAWASAKI Ki. 61/Ki. 100
No. 27–NORTH AMERICAN B-25 MITCHELL
No. 28–VOUGHT F4U - CORSAIR
No. 29–HAWKER HURRICANE MK. I-IV

ARCO PUBLISHING COMPANY, INC.
219 Park Avenue South, New York, N.Y. 10003